*There is still beauty here*

**There are no statistics**

**For this absurdity anymore**

*~ Angelo Letizia*

(excerpt from 'The moon's symbols' pg. 31)

## Recent Publications by Angelo Letizia

Letizia, A.J. (2024). Poetic Inquiry and Arts-Based Research for the Maintenance of the Republic and What Comes AfterA Vision for Metamodernity. Routledge

Letizia, A.J. (2020) Graphic novels as pedagogy in social studies: How to draw citizenship. New York, NY; Palgrave-MacMillan Press.

Letizia, A.J. (2018) Using servant leadership: How to reframe the core functions of higher education, New Brunswick, NJ: Rutgers University Press.

## Also, by Angelo Letizia

We Are the Winding Down
   Silver Bow Publishing 2022

Toward the Real: Poems for a New Reality
   In Case of Emergency Press 2022

Pilgrims of Infinity
   Silver Bow Publishing 2022

The Starry Devil and Other Unwanted Poems
   Silver Bow Publishing 2021

# There is still beauty here

## Angelo Letizia

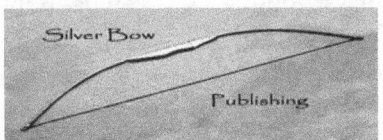

720 – Sixth Street, Box # 5

New Westminster, BC

V3C 3C5   CANADA

Title: 'There is still beauty here"
Author: Angelo Letizia
Cover Art: "Sundown Moonrise" painting by Candice James
Layout and Design: Candice James
Editor: Candice James

All rights reserved including the right to reproduce or translate this book or any portions thereof, in any form without the permission of the publisher. Except for the use of short passages for review purposes, no part of this book may be reproduced, in part or in whole, or transmitted in any form or by any means, electronically or mechanically, including photocopying, recording, or any information or storage retrieval system without prior permission in writing from the publisher or a licence from the Canadian Copyright Collective Agency (Access Copyright).

www.silverbowpublishing.com
info@silverbowpublishing.com
© Silver Bow Publishing 2024
ISBN: 9781774032862 book
ISBN: 9781774032879 e book

Library and Archives Canada Cataloguing in Publication
Title: There is still beauty here / Angelo Letizia.
Names: Letizia, Angelo, author.
Description: Poems.
Identifiers: Canadiana (print) 20240285875 | Canadiana (ebook) 20240285883 | ISBN 9781774032862
   (softcover) | ISBN 9781774032879 (Kindle)
Subjects: LCGFT: Poetry.
Classification: LCC PS3612.E79 T54 2024 | DDC 811/.6—dc23

*There is still beauty here*

**Dedicated to TRL, RRL & CBL**

*There is still beauty here*

# FOREWORD

Is there beauty in a grey sky? In an empty field or sewage plant? There might be beauty in these things, in the waste and bald tires, in the forgotten byproducts of our contemporary life. But beauty, like truth and meaning, is not waiting to be found, it must be created and fought for. Beauty requires effort- the perceivers and creators of beauty must put the work in. Sometimes, they might even have to die for it. But we, the creators and perceivers, are tired, we are exhausted, we are angry, bitter and resentful. It is easier to sit on the couch and forget infinity, easier to sleep. It is easier to hate than to love, easier to destroy than to create. I don't know if we as a civilization have what it takes to create the beauty we need to sustain us. We might just let the broken laptops and abandoned buildings overwhelm us, succumb to the progress and the oblivion and the chaos we helped engineer, let it slowly kill us because it is easier. The poems in this book, while not a definitive answer or philosophical statement, grapple with this idea, namely that we need to create beauty. I don't know how successful the poems are in this regard, and in some cases the poems may succumb to the couch, to the intoxicating nihilism. I'll let you, the reader, decide the fate of the poems; but in a wider sense, I will also ask you to decide if you want to create the beauty we so desperately need. If you do not, there is nothing wrong with that decision either.

Angelo J. Letizia, PhD
Manchester MD
December 2023

*There is still beauty here*

## Contents

There is still beauty here / 13

Your Truth / 14

January / 15

Do we have to be Real? / 16

I did what I was supposed to / 17

Instructions / 18

Who is to blame? / 19

Believe / 20

I cannot build home, bricks / 21

Insert it first / 22

Your systems / 23

Infinity sleeps / 24

Take back / 25

Kreis / 26

Useful / 27

The room in the room / 28

Letters in the forest / 29

There is no more water in the well / 30

God realized / 31

Desire / 32

*There is still beauty here*

The moon's symbols / 33

Hity ap, lop (because I can) / 34

I don't want TRUTH / 35

It's all there, all the time / 36

Too many Jesus's / 37

The surgeon's prayer / 38

A new language / 39

I don't know / 40

I wonder if / 41

There is beauty in the old carpet / 42

There is beauty / 43

The medicine doesn't fucking work / 44

Aaron and his ax / 45

Procurement / 46

Reality is a privilege but it makes me sick / 47

I never hated him / 48

There is nothing to achieve / 49

The old slaughterhouse was finally demolished / 50

I wonder if (2) / 51

Someone has to clean all of this shit up / 52

I'm sorry you can't walk / 54

LA3.03 / 55

Chronicles / 56

Eclipse / 59

All I want to do / 60

The things you don't notice / 61

Wake me up when the show is over / 62


Author Profile / 63

*There is still beauty here*

## There is still beauty here

Forget the old factory

And all its rust

Forget Maryland

And forget all the insults

Finally

you say to your sobbing daughter

"There is still beauty here"

As you mount the scaffold

## Your Truth

Your truth is peaceful

And transparent

Your success is oil

The electric furnace

Is logic

Temporarily

Obsolete saints

Do nothing but smoke cigarettes now

Everything you learned

Will

Soon

Be

wrong

## January

Scheduled thunder

And a broken January

They mark map

If you stay

On a platform

Addicted to residue

Truth is a syllogism

Or so

You thought

But logic

Is

Hilarious

If looked at

At night

*There is still beauty here*

## Do we have to be Real?

stars decompose

wash up on the shore

We don't need them

rusted out exemplars

Strewn in cold sand

Yawn, laugh

Because

They have died

And we are still real

## I did what I was supposed to

I clapped when

I was supposed to

At the well-dressed man

And his sad stories

I listened when

They asked for 7.5 million

I felt guilty

Because I wanted lunch

And the abandoned house with rodents

still existed

## Instructions

I think the stars are cold

I read

In my books

The desert is cold at night too

I think little lizards

Scurry

As the sun sets

I know autumn is cold

I know

the

desolate space

Is

hungry

## Who is to blame?

Are you to blame

For rotted corn

And the torn muscle?

Solar eclipse is your punishment

Invoices are the cure

The desert is an inscrutable theorem

Which you can't decipher

Open space is terrifying

But strangely

Still necessary

*There is still beauty here*

## Believe

Believe

Stars will be

Jelly

Soon

Pray trees will be

Clay

Drop the fire

Into this

Hungry room

And wait

To be

Nomads

    Again

## I cannot build home, bricks

I cannot build home, bricks

I cannot build car, oil

I cannot build a season, January and sadness

I don't create because I am not God

Just human

On a couch

In darkness

With cold spaghetti

And

Rusty fork

*There is still beauty here*

## Invent it first

Invent dirt, grass

Decompose

Invent red leaf

To give me peace

I built cold autumn air

Dream wet socks

Dream the floor

Dream the dream

Construct,

Light

To see this is all wrong

## Your Systems

Systems in desolate space

Where everything lives

Eventually

Constrain blank patterns

For

Descendants

So they can LIVE in those spaces

Slice vacancy and eat angles

Worms in disguise

Rat masks and

Colorful birds

Worm walks by

Worm in space

Dies as a homeless woman

## Infinity sleeps

Conjugate infinity to rape the terror so I can

Sing plastic

In the empty space

Between two trash cans cans

Sugar is fuel—>

And so is dust

Cling to schizophrenic stars

Heat cold

Sweats through another dimension

## Take back

Take back

Your goddam language

And its ridiculous apostrophes

Fuck your syllables

And germs

And all the stupid things

We are forced to share

Intersubjective plastic

There is no reason

For the

Lung anymore

No reason

For

*There is still beauty here*

## Kreis

Circular Octobers

Pulsate

A furnace, some type

Of heartbeat of an

Exhausted sky and

Grotesque abyss

Crawl    s

From the seat cushion, from

The water bottle

In

  To

## Useful

I want to be useful

To be

    An

Aorta

Hollow tunnel through

Warm space

To be

 An

Abortion

  Instead

She gave me cupcakes

Sugar

Hydrogenated oil, carbohydrates

Can be

   rearranged, errranged

Into a fetus

It's all the same stuff

So being useless

Is enough

## The room in the room

The room

Has red carpet

A plastic bird cage

With only plants

A small bottle of industrial lubricant

And a broken desk

Outside the hall is

A small linen closet

With flowered bed sheets

Above the garage

Lock the door

And sit

Close to the window

Smoke a cigarette

It's quiet

Where no one wants to be

## Letters in the forest

The dietician skillfully

Removed each of my muscles from

The tendon and bones

And placed them all in the forest

In alphabetical order

But the forest laughed

Because there is no alphabet in the forest

But the dietician went back to my apartment

And carried all my things.

Coffee maker, ripped couch cushions,

Rakes and old lamps

And placed them all on the forest floor

All these things

Became indistinguishable from my muscles

And the leaves

And the dietitian

Were finally happy

## There is no more water in the well

There is no more water in the well

It has been dry for some time now

The bicycle chain is rusted

There were some high importance emails

That he didn't answer

But it is no matter now

Somewhere, someone slowly strums

An old guitar

It is peaceful

And he can finally

Enjoy October

He can watch the leaves die

## God Realized

Stray dogs nibbled at a star

And God realized

The sky was only a potato peel

Without an answer

A kitchen table without

The idea of a kitchen table

But you have to believe in these things

To make them real

*There is still beauty here*

## Desire

I don't want

  To light the lamp

I don't want

  To let you hold my arm when you walk

I don't want to pray, or spell correctly

Or fix the ceiling

No

Let the trash pile up

And don't clean the toilet or dishes

Break every light bulb

Sit in the dark

And forget

All

Your

Promises

## The moon's symbols

The moon represents

Fabric and sadness now

And the hardwood floor

Is

A broken foot

Salute killers, persecute helpers

There are no statistics

For this absurdity anymore

## Hity-ap, lop (because I can)

Splace enters

Infinity


(why do you get to decide?)


Gklass is strength floor now


(were you there when the universe was created?)


No, so I can make this up


I don't wanna pick up the cards or push your wheelchair

I don't want to spell tihs correctly


I anwt .. I


A new arrangement

## I don't want TRUTH

I don't want truth

I want peace

I want silence because

All color is a lie

There are too many things

Too much paper and dust

Too many awards

I want to fail

So I can know

## It's all there, all the time

November makes me listen

To sad music

Desolate pianos

Ring across

Deserts and parking lots

On cold nights

I can't stop thinking

About what you did with him

I can't keep this knife at my wrist

I wish tomorrow

Was wrong

## Too many Jesus's

On each street

There is a Jesus

Some nailed to telephone poles

Stinking in the black wax

Mouthing default players

Another Jesus is strewn in a tree

Leaves circling around him

Like some grotesque autumn masterpiece

Jesus's arm stuffed in a mailbox

And his head ground

To jelly

By snow tires

I sat with another Jesus

Who smokes a joint

On a stranger's porch

We don't talk

But he stares off into the stars

He understands

What we need

## The surgeon's prayer

A surgeon

Cuts a star down

Every night

And puts each one in a box

I asked her why she was doing this

And she said, very matter-of-factly

Because we don't deserve the stars

We deserve a blank universe

Without stars and heat and sun

In the cold space

An egg gestates and

Is nourished by titanium

And waits to crack

And show us

Who we really are

## The new language

His eyes turn into fire

And his blood is a carpet

Each cell

Becomes plastic

A new savior is born

From the things of this world

And he was beautiful

And incomprehensible

So people jeered him

And crucified him

On a light post

But all the stupid people

Went back to the old churches

And prayed to the old gods

And waited

For something

That already came

## I don't know

I don't know

What the sun means now

We need a parking permit

To park the car

In some star

Build a saint

With sweet potato peels

And coffee grinds

Arrange all the scraps

Into something

We can love

## I wonder if

I wonder if

I could substitute blood for

A broken plastic cup

Or replace the old linoleum floor

With a cold November afternoon? Or a cloud?

Or a blood pressure pill?

Each diseased cell could be a library bookshelf?

It doesn't seem fair

That we have to live like this

That there is only one way

To be

## There is beauty in the old carpet

There is beauty in the old carpet

There is meaning in the rusted tin can

There is something worth saving

In the broken plastic cup

Believe there is beauty and meaning here

Even when there isn't

Pray to the residue in the oil furnace

And the caramelized soot

In the burner of the stove

These hieroglyphics can tell you something

As you contemplate hanging yourself

## There is beauty

Even in the ruins

Beauty

     In the empty          space

There is no east

And no west anymore

But we still pretend

That we know things

Three weeks ago

I was a little smarter

But now

I am more certain

*There is still beauty here*

## The medicine doesn't fucking work

You sold me placebos

And now I can't get a refund

But I can get revenge

I packaged infinity (because only I could see it)

Into little hard candies and weight loss pills

I quietly wrapped up the sun and put it in your reservoirs

To dissolve all your logic

And show you

How to die

Properly

Because you lived like charlatans

## Aaron and his ax

I want to brush my teeth with motor oil

And clean the windows with toothpaste

I have a special superpower

I can make you live like me

Dismantle logic like we took apart the door frame

To fit your fancy new fridge into the house

Disassemble every piece of the foundation

And unscrew every bolt

I can live in the debris and be king of this desert

There is beauty here, to me, in this wasteland

Of logic and old tires

But what would you do?

Fold up, cry on your expensive comforter

Which means nothing now?

Say a rosary?

You could never live like this

Using rocks as currency and

praying to the savior in the downed electrical wires

But I don't need a savior

## Procurement

The invoices

Give a strange comfort

A finitude

Like a corner

Or a simple equation

But you cannot achieve a planet this way

Or plumb the dirt

Of the garden in front of your home

But we need the dark

Not to know the light

But to know ourselves

And no number of invoices

Can tell us that

## Reality is a privilege but it makes me sick

Do I have to earn reality?

Earn the cars and houses and

Bits of hair and blood?

Each bone cell,

Do I have to crawl through fire

To claim

What everyone else gets for free?

This all must be earned (for me)

The only motion

Is earth

The only noise

Is the low static of the television

When the vacuum starts,

Jab the hose into my shoulder

Suck out the blood

And all the figures

I use for comfort

Suck it out and start again

If I have to earn reality

I don't want it

## I never hated him

I wanted to stab the stranger

As he passed me

My heart beat like Jupiter

Like that distant but terrifying planet

Memories are dust in the stars

I watched the stranger walk away

I never hated him

But he scared me

And this universe unfolded like a death certificate

On an office desk or

In your car

At six am

We haven't even slept yet

But

I saw the stranger again

## There is nothing to achieve

Consciousness

Is no achievement here

It is an alien

In the darkness

A strange anomaly

Which measures itself

In cancer and plastic

Consciousness is temporary

And won't know

When it dies

*There is still beauty here*

## The old slaughterhouse was finally demolished

I wrote a poem

A year ago

As I waited to pick up

My daughter from the dance

I wrote that humanity

Should stop fucking each other

And give the earth back to itself

I should listen to my own advice

I should never have fucked anyone

Because I am a shitty parent

For yelling at my other 9-year-old daughter

Because she slammed the door

But I do the same stupid shit

So how can I be mad?

At least I have life insurance

## I wonder if (2)

The president

Will let me create

A new language

I am tired of using

The same words

To describe

How irritated I am

Over the simplest

And stupidest things

*There is still beauty here*

## Someone has to clean all of this shit up

Eventually

All the broken porcelain

All the syringes and plastic

All the spoons and used condoms

All the markers of our progress

Someone quietly

And methodically will have to place

All this crap

Into a black garbage bags

While everyone else is passed out

But this job is not as bad as it seems

(I will most likely do it so

I can be there at the end

When the universe finally dies

I will be there

To clean up

Whatever is left

Maybe some dust

And chunks of planets

And, then

*There is still beauty here*

Finally

I can remember the line from the bible

And say I fought the good fight

Smoke a joint

And enjoy

The cold vacuum

## I'm sorry you can't walk

I'm sorry your medication doesn't work

And I'm sorry you're sick

At such a young age

It' not my fault

It's just bad luck

Or genetics or lifestyle

It's the reason

Why those who don't deserve to win usually do

It's the reason I don't believe in God

It's the reason I can never find the remote

When all I want to do is lay down

And look

The poem is about me again

## LA3/03

An old girlfriend

Once told me

To stop being such a Catholic

So, I didn't forgive her

And then I stopped believing in God

I wonder what she would think

But I saw that she was busy

At her kid's baptism

Fuck your metaphysical comfort

And fuck your salvation

At least I wasn't duped

For too long

## Chronicles

I filled up the gas tank

But ironically,

I was still empty and tired


I walked around the classroom

To read their stories of snowflakes

The little one said to me

"I like sad endings"

I asked her why and she said

"I like sad endings"

She gave me her snowflake

And I was finally happy


My only clue is a memory

A skeleton of something that dies

So I sift through the bones

Looking for proof that yesterday

That i

Still exist

*There is still beauty here*

Trees and stars step aside to form a path

They offer no sanctuary, I am alone

As I open the door to her apartment

I can't force the world to be real

Tollbooths, snow, trucks are echoes

In some nightmare

That I had coming home from work

I am afraid to get off the exit

I am afraid of the roads and restaurants and all

Of the evil things that surround me

One night, around a quarter to nine

In the snow, the world ended

Everyone vanished except me

i was alone on a planet I never asked for

Or even liked

I still filled my gas tank though

So I could drive around the dead towns

There is a certain sadness of daily life

At the bank, on the road

And I have to record it for some reason

*There is still beauty here*

I am so afraid that the mundane things of this life

The forks and hardwood floors

The wrapping paper and burnt-out laptops

Will rise up and murder us

Snow in the cold night is sadness

It cannot be written about

It cannot be confessed or mended

It simply is felt, in the dark, alone

## Eclipse

I have so much to do

I should hang the drywall

And start taking up

The stained carpet

Instead

I just sit

And watch television

And wonder if

The gods ever shirked their responsibility

And if one of them

Ever forgot

To light the sun

## All I want to do

Is listen to sad music

And think about my failures

The dead trees give comfort

In this regard

But their death is only temporary

The old slaughterhouse

I wrote about three years ago

Was finally bulldozed

And now,

I can be happy

*There is still beauty here*

## The things you don't notice

White delivery truck

And pump station number 4

Unauthorized personal

Keep out

Miles of pipes

Under the pavement

That trick or treaters

Will never know

Sewers and electrical closets

The space behind

Your oil furnace

Empty schools

And office buildings

Three crows

Fly at night

But you don't know

*There is still beauty here*

## Wake me up when the show is over

I lay on the couch

Because I am tired of infinity

And its lure

I want to watch the same advertisement

On the old TV

Sell me a medicine that does not work

I want to watch the same things

Over and over again

Leave me alone

And let me be saved

In the damp basement

## Author Profile

Angelo Letizia writes mainly speculative themed poetry and is a professor of education at Notre Dame College in Baltimore Maryland. His true passion however is poetry. 'The Starry Devil and Other Unwanted Poems' was his debut book of poetry, followed by 'Pilgrims of Infinity'; 'We Are the Winding Down'; and 'Toward the Real: Poems for a New Reality'.

His poetry has been published in Tales from the Moonlit Path, Bewildering Stories, The Atlantean, Sirens Call, Red Planet, Fevers of the Mind, Dissections, AHF Magazine, Lothlorien Poetry Journal, Bindweed Magazine & Bowery Gothic to name a few.

www.ingramcontent.com/pod-product-compliance
Lightning Source LLC
Chambersburg PA
CBHW071321080526
44587CB00018B/3305